Stowaway

For Sioned and Rhiannon.

Stowaway
A Levantine Adventure

Richard Gwyn

Seren is the book imprint of
Poetry Wales Press Ltd.
57 Nolton Street, Bridgend, Wales, CF31 3AE
www.serenbooks.com
facebook.com/SerenBooks
twitter@SerenBooks

ISBN: 978-1-78172-458-3
ebook: 978-1-78172-456-9
Kindle: 978-1-78172-457-6

A CIP record for this title is available from the British Library.

The publisher acknowledges the financial assistance of the Welsh Books Council.

Cover artwork: Abraham and Jehuda Cresques, Catalan Atlas,
Eastern Europe view from the South.

Author photograph: Daniel Mordzinski.

Printed in Bembo by Bell & Bain Ltd, Glasgow.

Contents

You'll always end up in this city. Don't hope for things elsewhere:
there's no ship for you, there's no road.
Now that you've wasted your life here, in this small corner,
you've destroyed it everywhere else in the world.

— C.P. Cavafy, 'The City'.

To a wanderer the faces of all islands
resemble one another. And the mind
trips, numbering waves; eyes, sore from sea horizons,
run; and the flesh of water stuffs the ears.

— Joseph Brodsky, 'Odysseus to Telemachus'.

Levantine cities are the future, as well as the past. Globalization means
we are all Levantines now.

— Philip Mansel, *Levant*.

Reckless Travel

Some journeys he undertook
with the certainty of eventual arrival.
Others, by contrast, he embarked upon
with little or no intention of ever
reaching any destination.
The term adopted for this
by his imaginary biographers
(who accompanied him everywhere)
was *reckless travel*. He became
adept at such peregrination,
of which the essential aspect
was never paying for a ticket.

Some Journeys

Some journeys never take you
beyond the point of departure.
This is what is known as
a fixed trajectory.

★

And once, you set out
on a journey
you did not complete,
and which has still not ended.

Stowaway I

He dreamed of Byzantium.

Once, when his boat was taken from him
and he could no longer abide dry land
he stowed away, for love of the sea.
They discovered him shivering in a lifeboat,
and he said to them: *Take me to your captain.*
He had no idea where the ship was bound,
but since boyhood had *dreamed of Byzantium,*
and so ... with no memory of boarding the vessel,
nor indeed where he had come from,
neither excuse nor explanation came to mind.
His appearance made of him the sea's orphan,
naked as he was; his violet eyes,
a garland of seaweed draped around his neck.
The captain looked him up and down.
I would put you to work, he said,
with a peculiar use of the conditional,
but he did not, at least not at once.
Someone brought a plate of small fish,
an offering of sorts. At orders from the captain
another sailor rushed away, returning
with a bundle of clean clothes.
He dressed where he stood.
He was waiting for the prophetic words to come,
as they usually did. But this time, nothing;
this time his shame was palpable:
he had lost the gift of speech.
The captain offered him a cigarette.
He smoked it bitterly, knowing all
that a condemned man needs to know.

Episodic Insomnia

Every night for a month he wakes
between three and four, perplexed by the routes
he took around the eastern Mediterranean years ago,
following sea-tracks or mountain paths
or those alleyways between tall decrepit buildings
that hide or reveal a dome or minaret,
glimpsing moments of a half-remembered journey.
Or else he is mistaken, and it is not the journey
that wakes him but the need to write about it,
and his alarum is this hypnopompic camel,
trotting over memory's garbage tip:
intransigent, determined. How is it
that we reach that state in which
the thing remembered merges with its remembering,
the act of writing with the object of that need
to tell and tell?
                        And so he wakes again
at a quarter to four, another dream-journey
nudging him tetchily into wakefulness
like a creature in search of its soul,
and this time he is peering from a terrace
on the milky heights at Galata, or else
gazing eastward from the battlements at Rhodes,
and wondering whether he has always
confused the journey with the writing of it,
whether the two things have finally become one.

The Names

I meet them in transit, in cheerless bars or dosshouses,
on canal walkways, in overgrown cemeteries.
Twitchy, sweating males; women following a dress code
from a fictional culture. Sun-streaked, matted locks;
army vests, cargo pants, pockets stuffed with dope
and string, pebbles, seaweed, chewing gum;
mouths poised in circumvention, never prone to the least
promiscuous truth-telling. Waiting for a dead dog alibi,
waiting, always waiting for drug deals never actioned.
At Saloníki station I watch them swigging wine from
plastic flagons; bodies crowd the marble floor.
And later, at the platform bar, there's one customer,
left ear missing, scraggy mongrel on a string. Talks
of *chicks messing with his head*. And without warning
slides from his stool like a sack of pans and comes to earth,
legs splayed, good ear glued to the ground,
muttering names: *Ananke, Mnemosyne, Antigone.*

The Days

The days are beginning to fold into one another, a slow-motion wing-beat on repeat. All those nights spent trying to sleep in railway station waiting rooms, a frantic collusion of rust, memory, a thousand miseries. Seagulls scratch at the window, their coarse sounds intended to lure you out. You drink tea and recall that you are bound by this anecdotal life, this song and dance, this merry lark. Outside there is a hunchback on the lookout for jailbait, or else an elegant octogenarian, holding out an enormous fish. Normally trees grow near such places, though by no means always larches. They signal an understanding between nature's routines and the need for perpetual renewal. An ancient chestnut, its roots ploughing through the soil like subterranean antennae towards the house and its foundations, eventually burrows beneath the building's skin. The tree and the house enter a symbiotic relationship, something like love, though it is the tree that has made the first move. In parallel fashion, two pencils lie across a yellow notebook on your desk. If you follow the direction of their points southeast for two thousand miles you will find the house and the tree: an exercise in style for someone desperate to believe in symmetries. Outside, you can sense the movement in the street without hearing anything or even looking. The day begins, as always, with a slow intrusion of medicated light; a rustling behind the curtain; the opening of a door, or a book.

Cities and Memories

Variations on a theme by Calvino.

When a man drives a long time through wild regions, his imagination begins to wander. *No, that's not right. Try again.* When a man drives across the last continent at night, from south to north, he must pass the mountain plateau of Omalos. *Oh please, not that. Once more?* When a man drives a long time across the dry plains of Thrace, he begins to wonder at the migrations that have marked this wretched zone. Turks, Bulgarians and Greeks, with varieties of cruelty and facial hair, wielding curved swords at one another's throats for centuries. Forced expulsions, exterminations, and the underlying terror that who you are, or who they say you are, is all a terrible mistake, merely circumstantial. And why, for that matter, are you not someone else? If only – you conjecture – I *were* someone else, and belonged to a different tribe, had a different shaped moustache or nose, the smallest detail of appearance and accent that matters beyond the value of a life. The Levant's legacy, never yet resolved: Greek, Armenian, Turk, Arab, Jew. I want to be friends with everyone, and yet know I must have enemies too, if only to maintain my friendships. What kind of crazy thinking is that? Saloníki, Smyrna, Alexandria, Beirut. We edge into new territories, in which boundaries are differently conceived and yet still intact. How do we progress from here to the next point, the next dubious epiphany? I feel at once as though we have been witness to a slow disembowelling, over many centuries.

Map of Venice

Here you are, deep inside the limbic system, the *calli* twisting into *campi*, both deceptively embroidered with story, every turning accompanied by a trio of blind violinists. No haven beneath the supercilious scrutiny of gulls: an exhausting labyrinth in which one false option leads to another, ending in a place where, truly, the sun never shines. You take a new turning, glance at the name-plate of the alley, which bears no relation to the name on your map, continue with a sense of desolate determination, having long ago lost all sense of an eventual destination, only to come across it unawares, as though the city had entered your bloodstream, laid a viral trap, and now was claiming hegemony. You are forever the victim of your own confidence in finding the way. You propose a direct route – according to the map, of course – only to find that the phenomena of stone and water get in the way, and you appreciate once again Calvino's notion that the city reveals only a possible version of itself, one of many. Later, seated by a canal, staring at the floating world on the side of an illuminated building, you come to another understanding: that what is being described in all these false turnings, darkened doorways, dead ends, abrupt descents to water, falsely proclaimed destinations, humorous asides and triple bluffs, is simply a map of yourself, or of anyone you care to name.

Stowaway II

He is put to work.

He is not put to death, but to work,
as the captain has forewarned,
which amounts to a type of slavery.
Not that the work is difficult; indeed
he has an aptitude for maritime tasks.
He scales the rigging *like a monkey*
and a deckhand cries:
him fly between the masts.
The crew stand below, eyes uplifted.
They gasp as he defies the claims of gravity.
A natural, the boatswain says.
But he is nothing of the kind.
Knowledge of his parentage
would terrify these humble souls.
He could make his special skills
work to his advantage, but arrogance
must be held in check. The stumps of wings,
the nascent horns, he can keep these secret
by force of will, just as he can summon
gills and flippers. But he mustn't *flaunt*.
He develops, when he can remember,
a feigned humility, which works well enough,
apart from the occasions when he takes wine,
and then he is inclined to boast, to abuse
the world of mortals, and speak ill
of their departed, the so-called dead.

Workers' Hostel

In Istanbul, a few months after the coup, walking the foggy streets of
Beyoğlu at dusk, seduced at once by the city's furtive sadness, its famous
hüzün, I enquired – in a run-down restaurant – after a room, and was
led, by a boy, to a working man's hostel. Never having entered such a
place, and ill at ease with my rudimentary Turkish, I was nonetheless
made welcome. Not a glimmer of the suspicion I suspected they might
bear. We sat in the lounge, TV blaring, glass after glass of apple tea,
exchanging cigarettes. I was shown my bed in a long dormitory, and
when I awoke at seven the next day the place was empty. All the men
had jobs to go to. I sat alone in the lounge with sweet tea, white cheese
and salty olives, wrote in my black notebook and smoked, until I was
told by the lame warden that he was locking up. I try to remember who
I am in this account: a young person with a weakness for symmetries;
a faded leather jacket, battered army rucksack, a change of clothes, a
lump of hash, a ball of string, and the knowledge that I must head for
Izmir, which once was Smyrna; an elusive memory that told me I had
something to uncover there, or retrieve.

The Cats of Aghia Sophia

The cats of Aghia Sophia are all of a breed;
possibly, like the founders of their palace,
a single family. Disdainful and dignified,
they wash and wash, never fronting up
to the audience. Sacred animals,
they know they are the object
of tourist scrutiny. Custodians of Byzantium,
their purpose is as lost as all that gold,
as certain as the collapse of Empires,
or overuse of the descriptor 'labyrinthine.'
The cats' names, which, tradition has it,
cannot be spoken, suggest an intricate history
of affiliation, of blood feuds, betrayal,
and the smoky perfume of metempsychosis.

Memo to Enrico Dandolo, Doge
of Venice, First Venture Capitalist

Wherever you are, back in the oyster shell of Venice
or else posthumously Canuting the celestial waves
with imperious gesture, I can only attempt
to impress on you, Dandolo, my shock at making
your acquaintance the other day,
in your monstrous sarcophagus.

I read of your whorish exploits in the name
of *La Serenissima*, only to find that after all
the thievery and carnage, you chose to be buried
in the very place you sacked.

I am as naught to Your Grace,
but between ourselves, History has not favoured you.
My friends and I cannot forgive the precedent
you set down for venture capitalists.
You'd like it here, in the twenty-first century:
we are all in it for the money, and the devil
— the one in the design and the detail —
always takes the hindmost,
chews them up and spits them out.
Some things never change.

Every city seeks its own shadow, just as every city
collapses into Byzantium, seeks itself in the labyrinth.

Stowaway III

Fitting in.

The vessel slices through the waves
and dolphins race alongside, leaping and diving.
He can make out their sounds, read their messages,
as they soar above the surf. He thinks it wise
to keep this knowledge to himself.
Sometimes the ship stops off at islands
or city harbours. The men go ashore and drink,
find women. Sometimes he joins them.
In Alexandria he is fellated by a myopic poet;
in Smyrna wins a monkey (dressed as the Sultan)
at a game of cards. In Beirut he smokes opium,
waking to find he has been robbed of his wages
and the monkey. Occasionally, he is happy.
He takes on the trappings of an ordinary seaman,
speaks in profanities, professes to superstitions
he does not hold. This lasts for a year or so,
as they traipse the Levant, from port to port,
from binge to binge, criss-crossing the ancient sea
until the map of his life becomes a matrix
of too many threads and he begins accumulating
sorrows, his heart made sore with all the miseries
that accrue from living among men.

Peter and the Ants

On the great island's ancient capital, I lived next door to Peter. Most mornings we would sit drinking in his shack, saying little, while he studied the behaviour of ants on the dirt floor. He told me he was training them. I dismissed this as the raving of an incorrigible inebriate. He was a perennial source of improbable explanations, fantastical stories. He tottered along the border between the familiar world and another, more tenuous reality. Then, one day, Peter came banging on my door, insisted that I follow him to his hovel, with its grubby whitewashed walls and corrugated tin roof. He left the door ajar, to let the light in. Thousands of ants were lined up on the floor, in perfect formation, as though practising drill. On close inspection I could see that they were marking time, beating out a rhythm with their tiny feet. Row upon row; column upon column. *Now watch*, said Peter. *Just watch.*

New Year's Journey

I

My wish that New Year's Day – to ride wild horses
over sunlit hillsides. What I got was misery, abandonment,
and chaos. I loved it, all the suffering and heartbleed,

humbling moments in the shadow of the God: and pain,
the haloed pain of tragedy – there was not enough that was enough;
it was never quite enough. And then you wanted more.

Trips through winter islands, marooned on Amorgos,
the ferry anchored to the island for a fortnight's storm,
and when we leave, young Nelson told us,

so long waiting, we will drag the island with us.
Islands, islands, each one with its secrets; each one viewed
through rain-swept glass in sea-lashed ports.

Kasia, Nelson, Declan and myself, with Kasia's babies
made a crew of six; the travelling winter circus.
Set a precedent, I told the others as we started out from Athens:

you see, a lot had happened in a little time, our heads were
full of Kasia's kidnap, articles of occult interest,
Artaud's madness, a girl who danced when she was sad,

and other ceremonials observed in a sprawling cemetery
at the city's edge, where the crimson paint shrieked
on the marble of her family vault: *Antigone, Antigone.*

On the boat to Paros, Kasia called for brandy *to feed my
Slavic soul.* I sniggered at such self-parody, as the ship
pitched like a drunkard through the January swell.

II

On Amorgos we slept rough, the Wicklow boy and me:
he had to cut his sleeping bag to make a spread for two.
I was wakened by a crone who screamed: *You'll die you'll die* –

and realised that we were buried in a snowfall. Frozen, we
huddled by that widow's woodstove, numb to any world beyond
our island, yet we had a mission raging in our blood.

In Paros on a shithouse wall I found more evidence, this time
attributed to Lorca: *I come from the countryside and refuse
to believe that man is the most important thing alive.*

And there it ended. Or ought to have. The final boat trip,
ticketless, we spent below decks, boozing with the crew,
and then returned to freezing Athens. Night that followed

sleepless night. What passed for mind so brandy-stained
there were submerged cathedrals in my eyes, songs
of drowning women in my throat. And then, one afternoon

I crossed Syntagma, and stopping at a signal felt a tug
upon the sleeve; an instant of impossible reflection.
I shuddered, knowing that my call had come before

My Time – and then moved on. The rounds of energy
that reckless travel requires were seizing up, and I retired
to a gloomy hostel, smoked in bed, read cold war thrillers,

evenings talking with a schizophrenic Samiot named George
who worked in a biscuit factory with forty Cretan women.
Barbarians! he sneered, *they all the time make play with me.*

Kasia and Nelson married, live in Warsaw, have six kids.
I passed the Wicklow boy years later, playing whistle in the metro.
His eyes were gone; what lay behind them also.

Stowaway IV

Rumours.

He had fallen into bad habits
taunting other members of the crew
and one night
when they had all been drinking
his comrades turned on him
and tossed him over the side of the ship
perhaps not intending him to drown –
more of a soaking, a lesson in manners
to which end one of them stood ready
with a life belt.
But after breaking the water's surface
and sinking a few feet down,
his body did not emerge;
the men began to fear that he had drowned,
and they would be held responsible
by the skipper, whom they knew
was well disposed towards the stowaway.
But he had not drowned.
Skilled as he was in shamanic arts
he turned himself first into a porpoise,
circumnavigated the vessel once (for fun),
a second time (to think)
and a third to finalise his plan.
He emerged from the water as a gull
and once on deck, a rat, scuttling
towards the men's quarters.
By the time the others had retired,
worrying among themselves
in their guilt at murdering a fellow-sailor,
they found him sleeping in his hammock,
dry and unscathed. From that point on
they treated him with caution,
and rumours began to circulate.

The Road to Susa

Variations on a theme by Cavafy.

You once took the road you had been warned did not exist, to Susa and the court of Artaxerxes, but discovered that you longed for all the things you'd left behind, in the other place. So you returned, and when a year or so had passed began to pine for Susa, her green river, her red cedars. And so it continued, from city to city, always wishing yourself in the place that you were not. Many years later, when you fell ill in Barcino, and returned home to Gwalia, you soon tired of its vile climate, its shaven-headed youths and shrieking harpies, and yearned for the cities of the south. But no man can choose the road not taken and keep his sanity, for always there is a place where he is not, and wishes to be, until such time as he finds who or what he is; and if the discovery does not geld him, only then will he wonder what else there is left to look for.

Maker of Golems

Our ancestors came from Girona
at the other end of the Great Sea
half a millennium ago.
Doubly exiled,
they built their lives from nothing,
served the Sublime Porte
providing woollen coats for
the Sultan's army.
When Sabatai Levi proclaimed
himself Messiah, they looked on,
sceptical at first, and then
believing, even to the point
of a third allegiance.
They were false *conversos*,
this time to Islam:
the three religions of the book
under their belts.
But my people were never truly swayed,
they remained constant
in their inconstancy.
They knew all such matters
were framed by language,
and a particular
application of the faith;
and they recognised another world,
alongside the visible,
in which none of their concerns
were of any consequence.

But the name *Sephardo* I bore with pride.
I made my way with care,
and an aching heart;
a question on my lips
that I could never quite articulate:
so many years in expectation
of some thing foretold, and
no idea if we were waiting

for a messiah or a monster.
In 1941 the monster came,
hauled our people in their thousands
on the black train to Birkenau.
But I remained, hiding out
with others in the mountain fastness,
an acolyte of nothing and of no one;
a seer, they called me,
and when I returned, unseen,
I was a friend to no one,
and found my vocation
as a maker of Golems.
Thus, in my small way
I became a custodian of nothingness —
reproduced our suffering
in men of clay;
like me, of no clear allegiance.

Earthquake

There was an earthquake. I sat in the village square and everyone came running. They ran from their houses and stood in the square. I had barely registered the first tremor when the second came, as we all knew it would. Being fifty miles from the epicentre we suffered little damage: broken crockery, the cracked glass frame of a fallen photograph of Venizelos, nervous cats. One week later I arrived in Kalamata. Tents lined the city park in rows, courtesy of NATO, and were occupied by the town's evacuated citizens. I walked the streets, sucked in the black, exasperated air. Nothing can be worse, said the man in the *ouzeria*. You cannot imagine an earthquake. You have to live it. It is the worst thing. His hand was trembling as he poured my drink.

Cities Unvisited

Although he never lived in Alexandria, he had read all the books. As a young man, he visited enough of the Levant to think he knew what to expect, and concocted the rest from Cavafy, Forster, Durrell and Pynchon. Sitting outside a café in the port of Paros he fell into conversation with a specialist in unforeseen events and together they dreamed up a delivery of illicit merchandise from Lebanon to Piraeus, with a storage facility on Cyprus. His interlocutor, a Russian who in former times had skippered a cruise liner, ordered champagne. It started to grow dark. Was it there, or somewhere else, that he decided he was never happier than in a Levantine port, as the sun goes down? Later, when he was the international figure of intrigue he was destined to become, he finally visited the city he had fantasized about so many years before. His disappointment was both intense and contradictory. Suffering suicidal thoughts, he experienced an epiphany: it was not Alexandria he sought but another city, a place that he would have to invent. This almost came as a relief.

Solace of the Journey

There is no solace in travel,
the Russian said –
always I am bored; and the anxiety
of preparation, standing in queues,
booking ferries, and spending time
with that class of globe-trotting fool
who has to engage you
in competitive conversation....

I was leaning on the ship's rails.
On the horizon I could make out
the minarets of the island.
I'll just take a small bag
and walk, I said;
try not to plan, find
solace in the minimal.
The less I pack, the less I have to carry....

True for you, the Russian said,
but I can never travel light.
I need to take my balalaika.
Add to that my memories,
my loves, my prejudices,
and my preferred means
of wasting time. How
can I fit all that
into a single holdall?

There was a ridge of cloud
hanging over the mountain.
I wondered how long
it would take to walk
from one end of the island
to the other.

Amorgos

I remember brittle winter mornings, holed up
in Amorgos, sleeping on a fishing boat,
octopus hung out to dry on a wire from stern to prow,
frosted skeletal spider webs, rubbery and wraithlike.
Twice I walked the length of the island
wrapped in a Greek army coat, fingerless gloves,
the recently deceased Russian's fur hat.
On one such walk I passed a dead mule, frozen
by the roadside, single mad eye glaring skyward.
I took it as an omen, but couldn't say of what.
A storm halted the ferry service for a week.
January stretched out across the snowy sea
and still my companions failed to show.

Facing Rabbit Island

That night we came down
from the colony on the hillside.
The afternoon had strewn
about our heads
a debris of hyperbole
and vague menace.
Bewildered before
the declaiming of Hikmet
by an Air Force General,
cast into stupor
by amphitheatre kitsch,
we sought out the solace
of the purple seaboard.
And there was something darker:
our path was convoluted
– the geography, as someone once
remarked, would not stay still –
and the road abandoned us.
A big white dog appeared, on cue,
led us to the village of Gümüslük.
Across a narrow stretch of sea
lay Rabbit Island;
I might have swum the strait,
but feared the straying tentacles
of confused sea creatures.
Everywhere was closed,
and what wasn't closed
was closing in. Fishing boats
rocked gently in the harbour;
the awnings of the restaurants
pulled down, dark and silent.
No movement in the street
besides those watchful cats.
I looked to our canine guide,
but he had slipped away.

No respite from the labyrinth;
it pursues you
even when you think
you have evaded it,
sucks you in deeper,
lets you wander, trancelike,
from one variety of despair
to another, presents you
with a chthonic version of yourself,
one that leads you back
at five a.m. to stagnant water,
the merciless mocking of the frogs,
the ironic moon.

Stowaway V

Jumping ship.

He jumped ship at Kastelli, and made his way
along the coast to Tavronitis. It was
the season of the grape harvest
and he found work with a farmer,
lay low for a month. His disguise
worked well, and he wore a hat
when the little horns began to bud,
as they always did in late September.
He treated them with olive oil
for they were sore. The stump of his tail
was another matter, and hurt like hell.
Nothing could salve it, until an old woman
from Sphakia produced a concoction
from the gizzards of the *fourogatos*
(an endangered species of wild cat)
and the tail receded inside his body.
The tourist season was dying
but he hit the Hania nightclubs
with the earnings from his farm work
and got talking with a pair of Germans, twins –
who invited him back to their hotel.
They tied him up, pleasured themselves in turn,
beat him with sticks, and urinated on him.
He was satisfied by this. He knew
deliberate self-abasement was
one of the routes to mystic truth.

Old Greeks

Those old Greeks, always waiting on some headland to
catch sight of a ship sailing in,
so as to celebrate a son's safe return (Aegeus)
or make good their strategy of murder (Aegisthus).
As a boy you too stood at Sounion's edge,
and ever since have seen those men in dreams,
waiting on a cliff, at the end of a pier,
or standing on the sea wall by Hania lighthouse.
There is one who remains there always,
with gulls screaming in attendance,
or without avian company.
He is smoking an unfiltered cigarette,
wearing a dark blue sailor's cap,
with plastic sandals on his feet.
He is waiting for a vessel that will bring him
to the edge of something,
where the familiar starts to lose its shape.
He stands out against the skyline,
a radical figure, confirming a belief
in the arrival of things expected.

Fisherman's Tale

Variations on a theme by Ritsos.

He sits by the window, smoking. Outside
a fisherman cleans scraps of kelp and mollusc
from his nets, toes poking through the weft.
The lighthouse is a white sentinel that caps
the breakwater. Hunched over coffee, he tells
the other men about the time he caught
a statue, an ancient bust trapped in his nets.
Someone or something put it there, he says.
He tells them he saw the perpetrator's back
and tailfin, her very long hair, how she was
laughing as she turned. It was at this time
of day, he says, gesturing toward the window,
the muted light, colours for which there
are no names. He knows they don't believe him,
but he doesn't care. He still has the statue.
Sometimes, at night, it talks to him, but he can't
make out the words. He remembers terrified eyes,
a crimson gash on upturned belly, sheen of light
on thrashing fin; the part of the tale he doesn't tell.

The Poet in Samos

Here are the things you left behind:
an old bus ticket to a place with an illegible name,
a stack of government files from distinct regimes,
a pile of rocks, a copy of Cavafy, well-thumbed.
I don't know how many meals you ate here,
by the seaward window. I don't know
whether the shutter kept you awake at night
as it banged unheeded on the wall, or whether
as you claimed, it was a kind of comfort.
Reading *Parentheses*, I see once more how
the world became an adjunct to your poems,
your poems an adjunct to the world.

Here are the things that you invented, even
as they, in turn, invented you. Nothing was inanimate.
You turned each movement of the head,
each falling leaf or bicycle into the fragment of a story.
You told us that you hid behind simple things
and if we could not find you, we'd find the things instead.

The Museum of Innocence

Back in Istanbul, he went to a place called the Museum of Innocence, where a famous author had created a mausoleum of spent emotion. There were piles of old stuff there, including an entire wall covered with fake cigarette stubs. He thought it was a shame to parade room after room of artefacts detailing a man's obsessions, his peccadillos, exposing to the world his phantoms of regret. Naturally, he fell in love with the guide and wondered whether the author had planted her there in order to entrap him.

Animal corollary

Walking on a coast road in another country, a dog joins him, pattering alongside: a large white dog with thick fleecy fur. He thinks he recognises the animal, from another time, from another life, it doesn't matter. It is an ally or a soul's companion, something he would find difficult to explain, but believes nonetheless. He feels the same about other animals, not quite randomly, and about certain everyday objects, without any evident connection between them. This must be the way the world is, he thinks, this coincidence of presence − animal and mineral. The realisation jangles for a while, wondering whether or not to make a home.

Only the Journey

He said he was not concerned with the lesser emotions, but never clarified what these might be. *Only the journey*, he would repeat. Only the journey *what*? I wanted to ask (but didn't). He expected us to complete the sentence in our imaginations, as though composing an alternative version of the Roy Orbison hit. Things went on like this for a while, his insistence on our understanding, our corresponding failure to understand. I began to see that some people never wish to be understood, only to be wondered at, or make of themselves a conundrum. He wanted the journey to mean something and yet not to mean anything, to constitute a life's enterprise and yet to have no *intention* attached to it.

Stowaway VI

Pine forests of the Aegean.

He wandered for days through
the Pine Forests of the Aegean
which descend through
gentle valleys to the sea.
He drank water from streams
and ate nuts, found shellfish
in the shallows. His plan
was to steal a small boat
and make for one of the islands,
thence to Piraeus
and there join another ship.
But he remained in Anatolia,
the days were balmy,
he had no need of money.
Once he wandered into a village,
found work in the melon fields.
In the evenings he sat with the old men
drinking raki. He spent a month there
and afterwards stumbled
through the forest, stupefied,
having forgotten all direction,
all sense of purpose.
His eyes hurt and his head ached,
his body was scorched. He climbed
up rocky slopes in an attempt
to reach a high place from which
to throw himself. The soft skin
of his wrists bled. His hormones raged.
He knew that no doctor could mend him,
no medicine appease this sickness.
Eventually, a great tiredness overcame him
and he slept for many days,
waking weightless,
without a care, but without a soul.
He made his way towards the city,
any city, looking for trouble.

Hospital Stay

He is convalescing in a Levantine hospital, from an injury he cannot remember incurring, one of a series of mishaps that befell him that bad summer, during a passage of poor performances, oral, sexual, pugilistic, drugs of an indifferent quality notwithstanding, not caring which, not knowing whose side to take in one too many battles. His hallucinations confuse and entertain, by turn. This time the singers line up outside his hospital room in formation, on a telephone wire, ready to perform a high-rise cantata or some such. Perhaps, he thinks, next time they might also juggle, or toss a dwarf; it could only improve the quality of the afternoon, low grey cloud piled thick like pleurisy. He has been given a small room off the ward, presumably so that his minders might monitor his behaviour as much as his wellbeing. Must have got in with a bad lot, as his father might once have said. Must have taken a knock. His throat hurts, but so does most of his body, with an intensity and persistence that render him inert and gurning. *Nothing is broken*, a nurse assures him, as soon as he regains consciousness and begins to ask questions. *Nothing is broken*, she repeats, using a Greek adjective that has always made him smile, but not this time.

Milk of Human Kindness

On any other occasion I might have felt trapped, claustrophobic, the victim of a kidnapping, but the room has a pleasant light and from the window I can see the rooftops of a city that might be Izmir, or even Beirut, but is probably neither. I have a vague memory of receiving death threats, a late-night pursuit through alleyways. Perhaps it will do me good to stay here and take stock for a few days. Let them look after me, let me lick my wounds, let the nice nurse come and bring me warm milk at night before I sleep, administer sedatives without which I would be in too much pain. I can hardly walk. Escape is out of the question. Besides, where could I go? *To the sea, to the sea*, as always, comes the reply, sung by a row of swallows perched on the wire outside the window. I catch glimpses of them as they soar and dive against the blue sky, stretching my neck to catch sight of cluttered roofs, TV aerials, satellite dishes, distant cranes; a place of arrival and departure, a city, like all ports, on the edge of things.

Terrible Dream

Still in his hospital bed, he wakes from a terrible dream in which his teeth have crumbled to powder in his mouth and his bones are dissolved, leaving his body a slack sack of skin and blood, a lame duck, a limp dick, a deflated balloon incapable of grasp or graft, but still with the potential for disastrous puncture. His mind, however, retains full consciousness: the definition of helplessness. Outside clouds heap thick against the skyline and the gulls make their raw, ugly sounds. How can the body sing when the soul has sunk this far? The body has its own rules, cannot be regulated. The presence of absence always so acute, it seems important to relegate thought (the teeth and bones) at the expense of emotion (blood, mucus, waste). The logic of this dream persists longer into the day than he might have wished.

The Spice Markets of Antioch

After escaping the asylum,
I had no choice but to endure
the desert crossing,
walking at night to avoid
other travellers,
sleeping in snatches.
I could speak to you of
the spice markets of Antioch,
but don't you weary of all this
second-hand exoticism?
In Tarsus a blind merchant
led me by the hand,
showed me the wine shops,
and pleaded with me
to share his bed. I told him
I was not inclined
to sodomy, that I preferred
the sweetly fragrant fig
to the throbbing stalk,
but I allowed him
to suck toothlessly on mine,
then smashed his skull in
with a builder's hammer
and took up residence.
He had a horde of silver,
which I distributed
among the destitute of that city
(well, some of it).
What could not be salvaged
from the blind man's dwelling,
I burned. After three days
I set off on my way again.

Taking root

'A rootless individual who takes root wherever he finds himself'★

He knows he cannot belong,
that he will always be a foreigner;
nor ever will be a true Levantine,
unless he puts down roots: a paradox.
So, he settles for a while
– he cannot think in terms of
a permanent arrangement – in Beirut,
meets a nice Christian girl,
who bears him five children in ten years,
all of them fine and strong,
and he enjoys the easy yoke (or so he sees it)
of work and marriage. With the stolen silver
from the blind man of Tarsus
he opens an emporium of herbs and spices,
which soon becomes a small empire
with shops in the Lebanon, Alexandria,
Saloníki, Istanbul. The Levant is his oyster,
and he builds the family home in Smyrna:
here there are fewer constraints on   .
his pursuits (libidinal and fiscal)
and he can direct operations from
a seat of privilege. He blasts several enemies
to make way for his growing enterprise;
charters camel trains; forms a private army,
bribing brigands into service
to ensure that traders
through the Caucasus pay his levies.
He breaks into dried fruit; dates, figs,
raisins, for the European market,
monitors the opium trade, and
commands a monopoly in time for

the morphine boom of World War One.
But he knows that on the horizon
hovers a terrible conclusion
to all that he's contrived to build.

* Definition of a Levantine, attributed to Georges Zananiri Pasha
  (supposedly the model for Balthazar in Lawrence Durrell's *Alexandria
  Quartet*) cited from Zananiri's memoir *Entre mer et désert* (1996) in
  Philip Mansell's *Levant* (2010: p.269).

On the Quay: Smyrna, 13 September 1922

The fire starts four days after Kemal's occupation. Flames leap high above the city, buildings belch black smoke; the air is fetid with the stench of burning flesh. Thousands on the quay are crushed together; a quarter of a million, by some accounts. At either end are soldiers with machine guns. Those who had once been neighbours are beating Greeks, Jews, Armenians – now become *the enemy* – with rifle butts, battering them with clubs or bars. He struggles through this heaving mass to the water, past old men and women, past children, past bodies screaming but inert against the human tide. By the harbour wall, the water grey with bodies of the drowned, he sees a rat, perched on a bloated floating form, chewing at its face. He plunges in, every stroke colliding with a body, adrift or sinking in the grey and burning sea; so down he dives, reliant on those skills that once saved him from his ship-mates, sinks deep into the waters of the bay before emerging, pristine, and swims with strong strokes to the steamers, picking out the one that flies the *tricolore*.

After Smyrna

*What you're left with is a lifetime of nostalgia, longing for what you've lost
and can never have back.* (90 year-old Greek woman remembers her home
in Anatolia, in BBC documentary on the Greco-Turkish war.)

Years later he'll watch footage of the evacuation: this was a time, he will
recall, when adults of both sexes wore hats, whatever the occasion, and
men smoked relentlessly. He sees them with their leather suitcases and
their Chaplinesque fast-motion walk, every one of them hobbled by a
disaster yet to happen, the smoke billowing behind them. These figures
pervade his thought whenever he discusses politics with his fellow exiles,
or listens to *rembetika.* He has learned what it is to be a refugee.

In Piraeus he meets others, from Trebizond and Cappadocia, places
where he has never travelled, but now begins to visit in his dreams. The
more Greek he is made to feel, the more he fights back, to become his
other: Turk, Jew, Arab, Kurd: he too is the one *out there*; the other loiter-
ing within. He hears the exiles' stories, sees them in his mind's eye, and
begins to understand that every narrative contains its opposite.

Incident in Rhodes

He boards a mahogany yacht, with red sails,
that covers the strait from Marmaris to Rhodes.
Disembarking, he wanders through the old town.
A couple of young Swedes, lounging on a terrace,
call him over; they laugh and proffer ouzo,
not knowing what a terrible mistake they
are about to make. He considers their blonde hair,
their long, tanned legs, their easy manner,
the waft of sex, and recalls the German pair
from Hania. What is it with these Nordics
in the south, every cool restraint wiped clean
with alcohol? It might be fun, he thinks,
after the horrors he has endured: the loss
of friends in battle, cholera-stricken towns,
Armenian heads impaled on poles, long nights
under a barrage of artillery from Kemal's lines,
the arduous retreat in hostile Anatolia,
his desertion and final descent through
pine forests to the Aegean coast,
and now release with these compliant Swedes?
But no. He smiles back at them; *another time,*
perhaps, he says; continues on his way.

Shabra and Shatila (September, 1982)

There were times when our lives
overlapped in Crete. From the start,
I was aware of – what to call them? –
his *special skills*. The time he spent away
in Lebanon (courting a Maronite girl);
his visits to a mysterious building in Souda,
where the U.S. 6th Fleet was based.
I was recovering from a mystery fever
in slovenly discomfort, at the house on
Gerasimou Street, geraniums in the little square
where the hookers hung out bedsheets,
and we'd spend evenings smoking,
with cups of mountain tea, as the gypsy kids
played football in the dust.
But in late July his girlfriend was killed
– victim of a bomb attack –
and he returned to Lebanon,
eventually serving with Hobeika in Shabra,
not out of loyalty (he couldn't conceive
of loyalty to a cause) but from revenge.
In Shabra he saw dead women
with skirts hoisted around their waists;
castrated teenage boys; pregnant women
with their bellies ripped to shreds,
murdered babies tossed on a garbage heap;
revenge on revenge, a massacre for a massacre.
Some victims were scalped, some had Christian
crosses carved into their flesh.
Most of them, no doubt, innocents,
just as she had been, his Céline.
This was the Levant he'd always known,
freed from its cage of tolerance and *dhimmitude*
driven by blood-lust, all notion of co-habitation
blown away: this was the Levant-to-be,
the millennial Levant that would come
full circle thirty years on, with *Daesh*.
He vowed never to take up arms again, in any war,
and certainly not in one not of his own making.

The Names: Remix

That winter, snow lay thick in Saloníki.
I was woken by a guard as we arrived,
having jumped a night train
expecting to be slung off
in the Athens suburbs. But my luck held.
The station waiting room was warm
and I dawdled there,
counted out coins for brandy.

At first I didn't recognize the vagrant,
rising from the marble floor,
as he stumbled to the bar
and took a stool beside me.
He led a mutt upon a string,
that slunk and sniffed about our feet.
Who can predict the passage of the years,
the bitterness of memory?

I greeted him: *Yasou*, friend,
long time no see – last I heard
you were boning cuttlefish for tourists in Euboea.
He took it badly, though it was meant in jest:
You thieving cunt, he said,
you stole my golden fleece,
drank my ouzo, fucked my girlfriend,
and now come speaking friendship?

I leaned over, as if to hug him,
but hey, things happen
if you carry a knife.
He slid to the floor, like a sack of spuds,
twitched, made gurgling sounds
as the blood pooled around him.
The dog circled, peed on his shoe.
Someone screamed. I beat a hasty exit.

I knew him when I was Sabatai Zevi,
preaching self-abasement
in the synagogue of the Marranos
and wore a crown of fire above my head.
He had betrayed me then,
as his kind always will.
I found my way to the Kapani market
and vanished there, without a trace.

From Naxos to Paros

Of the journey from Naxos to Paros
all he could remember
were the lights of one harbour
disappearing into the black sea
and the lights of another
emerging from the same black sea
and he thought for a moment
that all journeys were like this
but that many were longer.

On Lesbos (November, 2017)

Washed up on Lesbos, he recognises
the familiar debris of retreat and exile,
wailing children, women at their wits' end
wondering, even now, despite the horrors
they have witnessed – the seared bodies,
grandmothers weeping in the ruins,
the harrowing desert trail –
if they ever should have left their homes.
Some are sleeping beside a vast heap
of deflated dinghies, life jackets, rubber rings;
a few male stragglers, as always, caught up
in mischief and thievery.
Another paradox:
he has seen this suffering before,
in Smyrna and Beirut;
the deportation of the Saloníki Jews,
the massacres of Shabala and Srebenica,
and after passing through indifference
has – to his own surprise – acquired
a quality akin to empathy.
He stays a few weeks, drives a jeep
into Mytilene for provisions, and
on one of these excursions
is queuing to buy medicines
at the pharmacy, when he recognises
a Syrian woman he knew
centuries before, in Aleppo.
She has barely changed, despite
the pall of fatigue around her eyes.
Amena, he calls out;
the woman turns, returns his gaze,
wondering who this stranger is
that knows her name, why he stares so,
with that intimacy granted by
the frail co-ordinates of war,
and with the air of one for whom
no harbour signals home.

Acknowledgements

Versions of some of these poems have appeared in the following publications: *Poetry Wales, Poetry Review, And Other Poems, New Welsh Review, The Harlequin, Wales Arts Review, New Boots and Pantisocracies, Periódico de Poesía* (Mexico), *Buenos Aires Poetry*, and *Otra iglesia es imposible* (Argentina): several poems appear in the bi-lingual collection *Ciudades y Recuerdos* (Mexico DF: Trilce, 2016).

The seeds for what was to become *Stowaway* were planted in discussions with Bill Herbert about Byzantium, the Ottoman Empire, and the Great Island, over the course of two translation residencies in Turkey, for which thanks are also due to Alexandra Büchler and *Literature Across Frontiers*. My research into the Sephardi was re-kindled by conversations with George Szirtes in New Delhi. Many thanks to Patrick McGuinness for his encouragement while guest editor at *Poetry Review*, and to Ailbhe Darcy and Damian Walford Davies for their comments on drafts. Amy Wack, poetry editor at Seren, has offered enthusiastic support from the outset. Warmest gratitude, for everything, to Rose.

Other books by Richard Gwyn

Poetry

Walking on Bones (2000)
Being in Water (2001)
The Pterodactyls' Wing: Welsh World Poetry (Editor, 2003)
Sad Giraffe Café (2010)

Translations of Poetry

A Complicated Mammal: Selected Poems of Joaquín O. Giannuzzi (2012)
The Spaces Between: Poems by Jorge Fondebrider (2013)
The Other Tiger: Recent Poetry from Latin America (Editor, 2016)

Fiction

The Colour of a Dog Running Away (2005)
Deep Hanging Out (2007)

Non-fiction

The Vagabond's Breakfast (2011)